Where Do Clouds Come from?

Weather for Kids (Preschool & Big Children Guide)

Speedy Publishing LLC
40 E. Main St. #1156
Newark, DE 19711
www.speedypublishing.com

Copyright 2016

All Rights reserved. No part of this book may be reproduced or used in any way or form or by any means whether electronic or mechanical, this means that you cannot record or photocopy any material ideas or tips that are provided in this book

Take a look at the blue skies. What do you see? What are these things floating in the sky? Do you want to touch them? They are clouds. We will talk about them in this book.

Do you want to know about clouds? Let's find out how clouds are formed.

A cloud is a group of small droplets of water. They collect around dust particles in the atmosphere. These droplets are from the water vapor which rises from the oceans into the atmosphere and they are very tiny so they can float. That is why it is said that water can exist everywhere in the surface of the Earth.

The atmosphere has clouds. All planets in the solar system with atmosphere have clouds in them. But places like the moon, that don't have an atmosphere, don't have clouds.

The water vapor rises due to the sun's energy. As the warm air rises, it expands and cools. Then the vapor condenses in the cooler air in the atmosphere. Interestingly, the cool air in the atmosphere cannot hold as much water vapor. For this reason, the vapor condenses. It forms tiny droplets of water which float in the air. The tiny droplets attach to a little bit of dust or some other substance, and now it is ready to become a rain drop.

How are clouds formed? Would you believe that the air can hold water? Through the process called evaporation, a gas is formed. This is called water vapor. As bodies of water are hit by sun's energy, the top layer evaporates. The water vapor is formed and rises in the atmosphere to form clouds.

When the water vapor from the surface of the Earth rises into the atmosphere, it condenses and becomes visible tiny drops of water or ice crystals.

Let’s Explore Further!

Water is floating around us. Yes, all the time water is everywhere. However, the water is invisible. The water is in the form of very tiny gas particles known as water vapor. That is why we can't see them. They are there but they are invisible. Along with the vapor are the tiny particles known as aerosols. They are the salt and dust floating around in the air.

The water vapor and the aerosols bump into each other in the atmosphere. Water vapor sticks to the aerosols when the air gets cooler. This is called condensation. The water droplets combine together and clouds are formed.

Most clouds are formed in the lowest part of Earth's atmosphere. It is called the troposphere. However, clouds can be seen as high as the stratosphere or the mesosphere.

Clouds are capable of holding millions of tons of water. Wow, Fantastic! Clouds come in different types. The main types of clouds are the stratus, cumulus, and cirrus clouds.

Why do clouds float? Clouds float even though they are made up of liquid droplets of water. Clouds float because they are warmer than the air below them.

Billions of droplets combine together to form a cloud. Clouds are moved by the wind currents. The wavelength of the ice crystals or water droplets combine to reflect a white light. That is why clouds appear to be white.

However, clouds may change from white to a dark color. This happens during a storm. As the clouds become thick and very compacted, the light from the sun cannot get into them. This makes the clouds appear gray.

As the air gets warmer, more water vapor is held by it. As the air rises, condensation happens which will eventually form clouds.

Clouds appear to be white. It is because sun's light is reflected by the clouds.

Storm clouds or cumulonimbus clouds can produce lightning and harsh weather such as tornadoes and hail. These clouds can be the reason why flights are delayed.

The beautiful clouds greet us in each new day. By understanding how clouds are formed, we get to know that everything in the world has its reasons and means for existing. In conclusion, everything on Earth has meaningful connections. The rivers, the seas, the oceans, the atmosphere and everything around us are interrelated. You and I are part of these connections.

Visit

BABY PROFESSOR
EDUCATION KIDS

www.BabyProfessorBooks.com

to download Free Baby Professor eBooks
and view our catalog of new and exciting
Children's Books

www.ingramcontent.com/pod-product-compliance
Lightning Source LLC
LaVergne TN
LVHW060513170826
845677LV00026B/1730

* 9 7 9 8 8 6 9 4 4 5 1 7 9 *